New Appi to Ministry with Older People

by
Arthur Creber
Assistant Curate at St. Peter's, Rickerscote, Stafford

GROVE BOOKS LIMITED
Bramcote   Nottingham   NG9 3DS

CONTENTS

THE COVER PICTURE

is by Peter Ashton

THE AUTHOR

Arthur F. Creber is Assistant Curate at St. Peter's Church, Rickerscote, Stafford. Prior to his ordination he was Director of the Beth Johnson Foundation, a charitable trust based in Stoke-on-Trent whose aim is to improve the quality of life for older people.

ACKNOWLEDGEMENTS

What is written in this booklet has been distilled through my work with older people, both in the Beth Johnson Foundation projects and in the parish of St. Peter's, Rickerscote, Stafford. I am grateful to all those who have shared with me something of their experience of growing older and have helped me think through my own attitudes to old age. I remain especially thankful to those who have taught me to think positively about the future.

My wife, Jeanette, pushed and prodded me into recording some of the work we have been involved in at St. Peter's. She also typed the text from my terrible handwriting. I am very grateful for her enthusiasm, encouragement and energy—we hope that our experiences here might result in many new initiatives being taken by the Christian Community to the benefit of an increasing number of older people.

A.F.C.

First Impression September 1990

ISSN 0144-171X

ISBN 1 85174 157 7

1. INTRODUCTION

Jim has Fallen Again

'May will not be coming today, Jim has fallen again'. May was to have been sidesperson that morning. Jim has Alzheimer's Disease. May and Jim were both active members of St.James' at one time, attending both morning and evening worship, now May comes alone. At one time they prayed and read the Bible together, they supported each other in their love of God and his word, now May prays and reads alone. Jim is unable to understand what is going on, he rarely remembers May's name. The joyful relationship and the sense of interdependence they once knew has gone and although May dare not acknowledge it, she is bereft. May and Jim are in their late seventies.

Beginning to Discover New Purpose

Joan 'does the flowers' at St. James. She leads a team of women who meet each Friday in the choir vestry to sort and arrange. Now Tom comes with her, he sits and watches, 'He's got nothing else to do on Fridays and would rather be with me than sit at home'. Tom is in his sixties, until retirement six months ago he was responsible for training craft apprentices at numerous companies across the area. It's been a difficult time of readjustment for both Joan and Tom, but slowly Tom is finding new opportunities for service within the church and in the local neighbourhood. He has been authorized to administer communion to the housebound. He has developed his ministry as a Reader and assists the chaplain at the local hospital. He is beginning to discover new purpose and new satisfactions after a significant loss.

These two stories, which are based on fact, illustrate some of the dilemmas which any of us could face us as we grow older. They also illustrate the challenges facing Christian Ministers and the church in general as we begin to come to terms with an ageing population. Half the people who have ever reached the age of 65 years in the U.K. are alive today. There are almost 10 million people over pensionable age in Gt. Britain, more than the number of children at school. Half of the population is over 50.

At the turn of the century only 6% of the population were over 60 years of age—there has been a massive population change during the first 90 years of this century.

A baby boy born in 1901 could look forward to 48 years of life and a baby girl to 52 years. In 1981 their life expectancy would have been 70 and 72 years respectively. This is a direct result of the improvements in medical care, sanitation, housing provison and nutrition.

But who are the Old?

In modern societies older people are more often than not defined in chronological terms; by the length of time they have lived. This way of deciding who is old is commonly linked to the statutory retirement age; in this country 60 for women and 65 for men. So, in our thinking, people over these ages pass into old age.

Defining old age chronologically has massive implications for how we view our older people, and for how they begin to perceive themselves in relation to the rest of us. For a start there is a change of status from worker to non-worker, then there are the questions of dependency and of their usefulness to society.

Defining old age in purely chronological terms simply reflects the cultural norms or mores of a particular society, as it does when we classify any period of life by this means (e.g. childhood, youth, middle age). The time at which people become old using a chronological measure varies throughout the world. In pre-literate societies people are regarded as being old at much earlier ages than in 'modern' societies. Using chronological age to signal the start of old age is, however, a relatively recent development.

The World Health Organization has suggested that 'the elderly' are 60-74 years of age whilst 'the aged' are 75 years and above—but again these are purely arbitrary distinctions. They bear little relation to the actual physical, mental or social health of individual people, as we all age differently and at different rates.

The danger of using chronological definitions is that they 'distance' us from people; we begin to think of groups of people in terms of the categories we fix. Looked at with other spectacles people over 75 years need not be 'aged', any more than those between 60-74 years need be 'elderly'. The way we think of people will determine how we minister amongst them. Chronological definitions are only useful for establishing demographic trends.

A different way of looking at ageing
A much more satisfactory way of thinking about ageing is to consider it within the framework of the human life-cycle rather than solely in chronological terms. The idea of an individually unfolding life-cycle is not new of course, Shakespeare spoke of our lives as the Seven Ages of Man in *As You Like It* and Psalm 139 speaks of the evolving continuity of our lives through various stages of development. Within this framework of understanding we are able to examine the different influences which shape the lives of individuals or groups of people, and so to respond to their needs in a much more constructive way; giving weight to the whole history of their lives.

The life-cycle approach shifts the focus from definitions of old age to creating descriptions of a person's history, growth and development. It is vitally important for those in Christian ministry to consider the life-cycle of each individual, rather than to respond to older people purely in terms of their age.

Birren (1960)[1] in seeking to clarify the components of an individuals life-cycle breaks down the ageing process into three categories:

i. Biological Ageing
> This he describes as the progress a person makes along his or her personal life-span as measured by physiological factors. It is concerned with the biological processes at work in us but also with the

[1] J. E. Birren, 'Ageing; Psychological Aspects', in the *International Encyclopedia of the Social Sciences* Vol. 1, Macmillan Free Press (p.176-186).

4

environmental factors which have borne on a person and which have limited their physical progress.

ii. Psychological Ageing

This is the way in which people grow to perceive themselves in relation to others. Our perception develops and changes over the years and as a consequence our personal behaviour and life-style is altered and modified. Psychological ageing involves such things as cultural influences, educational influences, individual emotions, temperament and social behaviour.

iii. Social Ageing

This relates to the social habits and behaviour a person adopts to fulfil the social roles and expectations of the society in which he or she is set.

The three categories, Birren explains, are not mutually exclusive; there are overlaps and interactions, but they will all operate within the individual's life-span.

The life-cycle approach provides us with a much more acceptable framework in which to consider the needs and potentialities of older people. It helps us draw together the threads of a person's life. It enables us to be aware of older people as whole people and lessens the likelihood of us treating them as a race apart, somehow detached from us by their years.

Older people in the Churches

A recent national survey showed that 25% of the people who worship in our churches are over pensionable age and that the ratio of women to men in this group is 4 : 1. We need then to think whether we are making an adequate response in our churches to the shift in population and to the numbers of people over 60, particularly women, who worship with us.

This is especially relevant as the one piece of research done on attitude change amongst older people indicates that we become more conservative as we age and prefer to maintain the *status quo.* Such attitudes help us keep our lives in perspective, they help us keep in touch with our roots, but they also make us more resistant to change. The loss of buildings, especially those with personal significance, like houses, churches, and public houses, arouses enormous emotions in us as we grow older, since they break the continuity with the past which gives a framework to our lives and helps us understand what has shaped us as individuals.

One of the difficult things about growing older is coming to terms with a multiplicity of losses—loss of ability to earn a living, loss of status, loss of some physical abilities, loss of friends and family members. The loss of continuity with our past can hurt as much as any of these, and the loss of churches or familiar patterns of worship can often result in feelings of bereavement. We are not prepared in earlier life for the accumulating losses we will experience later and so we interpret them as a rejection. For some, the losses in later life come very quickly, and there is not enough time between them to allow for healing through the grieving process.

Those who are making changes to buildings or styles of worship do not always recognize the level of bereavement being experienced and fail to see it in the context of the other losses of later life; they often fail to give the time or the space for the grieving to be expressed.

2. AGEISM

Ageism, is the word used to describe a blatantly discriminatory attitude towards older people. It can be seen in the way older people are stereotyped in the media, older men are often portrayed as cantankerous (e.g. Alf Garnett or Grandad in *Bread*) or useless and roleless (e.g.*The last of the Summer Wine*). Older Women are more often than not shown as silly (Dot from *Eastenders* or Edna Everidge's bridesmaid Madge Allsop) and sometimes as eccentric (Miss Marple) or wicked, with connotations of witchcraft. Our language also reflects our negative attitudes to old people e.g. 'old biddy'. More seriously the negativity we attach to old age can be seen in housing policy and employment practices and even in social welfare and healthcare provision e.g. the least qualified and most inexperienced Social Workers are inevitably allocated to older people. Ageism is found in every walk of life, imposing crude and arbitary restrictions on the lives of millions of people—just because we consider them old.

The recent T.V. programme—*Waiting for God*—relies for its humour on the unexpected challenge by some residents of a home for older people on the negative attitudes towards them, with which they are expected to collude. The confrontations are engaging and funny because they are in sharp contrast to the attitudes we expect from older people, particularly in the setting of a residential home. Full marks for the script writers!

Bernice Neugarten recently completed a long term study of more than 2,000 people in the U.S.A. between the ages of 70 and 79 years.[1] One of her conclusions was that stereotyping has increased hostile attitudes between age groups. She believes that we adopt negative attitudes to older people to separate ourselves from them:
> 'So long as we believe that old people are poor, isolated, sick, unhappy, confused, useless, rigid and reactionary . . . we can remain separate from them and relegate them to inferior status.'

The resulting harm, Neugarten believes, is great in terms of their perception of themselves, their activities and potential.

Whenever individuals or groups of people are labelled by society, they begin to asssimilate the assumptions behind the label, whether or not these assumptions bear any resemblance to reality or not. So the prevalantly negative view of older people held by society at large has been assumed by older people and is reflected in their own descriptions of themselves. Older people think they are of no value and by a variety of crude or subtle ways express this.

The following quote from Psalm 31, if not written by an older person, certainly shows some of the feelings of rejection felt by many older people, and what is more, because ageism is prevalent, we have assumed it is right for them to think like this.

[1] B. Neugarten, 'Grow Old with Me! The Best is Yet to Be', in *Psychology Today*, Dec. 1971 (p.45-48).

'Take pity on me, Yahweh,
I am in trouble now.
For my life is worn out with sorrow,
my years with sighs,
my bones are wasting away,
I am loathsome to my neighbours,
to my friends a thing of fear.
Those who see me in the street
hurry past me; I am forgotten
as good as dead in their hearts,
something to be discarded.'

The Search Publication *Against Ageism*[1] lists seven myths about old age
which affect people's thinking:
  i *The myth of chronology*
     —that people are 'old' simply by virtue of the length of their life.

  ii *The myth of ill health*
     —that all older people are in need of medical treatment.

  iii *The myth of senility*
     —that the intelligence of older people deteriorates with age and very
     many suffer from senile dementia. (In fact only 5% of people over
     pensionable age suffer from senile dementia).

  iv *The myth of isolation*
     —that all older people are lonely and isolated.

  v *The myth of misery*
     —that all older people are unhappy.

  vi *The myth of unproductivity*
     —that older people are incapable of making a useful contribution to
     society, they lack creativity and are redundant to the real future.

The major factor underlining the negative view of old age and which feeds
ageist attitudes is the fear of death. Many feel that ageism is part of a
collective and personal defence against our own demise. Piner (1979)
puts it like this:
   'It is death that haunts and fears us. The old have appeared to be its
   visible symbol and so have become our enemies. We have shrouded
   age in myths and stereotypes so as to hide our own deep fear and
   prejudice.

If this is the case, and I think it is, then the implications for Christian ministry both for older people but also for anyone at any other point in their life
cycle are extremely significant. Surely the Christian gospel has at its very
centre the message of victory over fear and death and is concerned to
bring release to those bound by the chains it brings?

[1] J. Darwin (ed.), *Against Ageism* (The Search Project, Newcastle-upon-Tyne).

The Church and Ageism

What position does the church take on Ageism? Does it challenge the negative view of old age or promote the same stereotypical images as the society in which it is set? I know of no empirical research on this, but my own deliberate and conscientious observations lead me to conclude that Christians have allowed the world to squeeze them into its mould. The church has failed to attack the myths and the underlying fears which cause older people to be pushed to the margins of our thoughts. It has failed to examine its own prejudices towards older people and has perpetuated a negative view of old age.

The language of Christians when talking about older people is indistiguishable from that of society at large, and commonly older people are quoted as being the reactionary forces in our congregations. The often quoted statement from the Bishop of Durham's enthronement address, that Charles McGregor was 'an imported elderly American', is packed with ageist assumptions.

The church has adopted the youth culture; evangelistic efforts inevitably have special Youth Nights and Youth Outreach but rarely include any special outreach events specifically for older people. Dioceses employ Youth Officers and in some cases elaborate programmes for young people have been established, but I know of no diocesan structure for assisting ministry to the increasing numbers of older people.

The 1988 National Evangelical Celebration (NEAC) included in its draft programme of workshops on Social Issues the following:
    Acting on the north/south divide
    Acting on unemployment
    Acting on racism
    Acting on the elderly
All the workshops in the series were to look at problems which bear on particular groups of people, except one. which was to look at people who are a problem! That's ageism—and it is rife in our Christian thinking.

Surely one of the most important aspects of Christian ministry with older people is for us to examine our own attitudes to old age and to the fear of death. We need to confront our own prejudice and fears and become confident of the victory over fear and death which is in Christ Jesus.

I will consider in the final chapter how we might challenge negative attitudes and also set out a number of practical ways in which Christians can undertake outreach to older people. But first we need to consider another fundamental question—just what do Christians believe old age is in God's plan for human beings?

3. APPROACHING A THEOLOGY OF OLD AGE

In spite of the recent attempts to come to a better understanding of human ageing and given that there is now a considerable amount of literature provided by the human sciences there is still, for the Christian, a fundamental problem—just where does ageing fit in with other aspects of our theological understanding of human existence? There are to be frank, few theological frameworks within which we can explore what ageing means.

The problem is serious for Christians working with older people, whether they be clergy, doctors, or social workers because without a coherent understanding of what we consider ageing to be in the will and purpose of God then our 'caring' can degenerate to a response to a few vague value judgements.

Kasterbaum, puts the question well, 'What does life mean if it replaces youth with age?'[1] It is my belief, after many years of working with older people that this question is not far below the surface of most people's thinking in later life. It is a question that the human sciences do not address and sadly the theologians have, by and large, avoided.

Many contemporary commentators have suggested that old age in this country is now simply a 'liminal' period, that is a period of life without a socially prescribed status. Our ageist attitudes may have pushed us to this, but does this mean that old age lacks meaning, is it just a waiting time, just a preliminary to death?

What has the Christian theological tradition to say about human ageing? Well, not a great deal! There has been a distinct lack of interest in the topic. Martin J. Heinecken[2] writes: 'There is no special theology for the ageing. There is only one biblically and confessionally based theology which is applied to the problems of adults'. In other words any questions which arise about ageing or older people are answered out of the basic Christian theological understanding of human nature, rather than from a specific viewpoint. So what little is said about ageing in the historic Christian literature varies widely. Christian thinkers have not been of one mind about what old age means in the purposes of God.

Having said this, Brynholf Lyon[3] in his book *Towards a Practical Theology of Ageing,* identifies three stands of thinking which appear to emerge from the literature.

  i Old age as a direct (individualistic) blessing from God.

  ii Old age as a period for growth, especially in our spiritual life.

  iii Old age as an opportunity for witness based on our personal experience of God.

[1] R. Kasterbaum and R. R. Hellerich, *The Church's Ministry with Older Adults: Its Theological Basis* (New York 1976).
[2] R. Heinecken, 'Gerontology's Search for Understanding' in *The Gerontologist,* (Sept. 1978), p.60-61.
[3] K. B. Lyon, *Towards a Practical Theology of Ageing* (Fortress Press, Philadelphia, 1985).

9

When considered together they stand in sharp contrast to the negativity of the prevailing attitude of our age but nonetheless they need critical examination.

(a) Old Age as a blessing from God

God, it is said, gives long life as a particular blessing to some, but why some should receive the blessing and not others is not easily understood:

'A hoary head is a crown of glory, it is gained *in a righteous life.*'

(Prov. 16.31)

(Hoary head is a synonym for old age in scripture)

'Honour your father and mother that your days may be long in the land the Lord your God gives you.' (Exodus 20.12)

At times the idea of blessing seems to confer on older people a very special place in the created order:

'You shall rise up before the hoary head, and honour the face of an old man, and you shall fear your God.' (Lev. 19.32)

This 'blessing' has however, always carried with it a tension, in that a long life involves physical and in some cases cognitive weakening. In any case very many people who have not led righteous lives, or honoured their parents have lived long lives.

The tension has led to some interesting theological contortions as people have sought to uphold the claim. What's more, some scriptures mock the idea of the blessedness of old age mercilessly (Eccl. 12).

(b) Ageing as a period for growth

Augustine writes:

'Innocence will be your infancy; reverence your children, patience, your adoloscence; courage, your youth: merit, your manhood: and nothing other than venerable wise discernment, your old age'.

Here the theological interpretation of old age is one of advancement progress, growth. The precise nature of this process, the terms to describe it and the articulation of its goals have varied considerably, yet there is an underlying consistency in the arguments. They are usually set out in this way:

The power of the body wanes, the pursuits of youth and adulthood become increasingly difficult to maintain as time passes, however, certain aspects of our life continue to have the potential to reach their peak.

Commonly these aspects are related to the spiritual life. In some expressions of the argument bodily decline is even seen in positive terms, it means a release of the person from the passions of the flesh to increase concentration on the spirit.

Fulfilment in old age then, rests on the appreciation of the proper subjection of the passions of life by the ageing process, so that other less tangible aspects of ourselves might be enhanced. Old age is seen to be a time of growth or advance, but only of the soul.

St. Paul's is perhaps the most commonly quoted text relating to this, he stresses the possibility of growth in spirit even though there is deterioration in the body:

'Though outwardly we are wasting away, yet inwardly we are being renewed day by day' (2 Corinthians 4.16)

I know many older people who could not accept that later life and their understanding and friendship with God should simply be reduced to a spiritual relationship with God through prayer, and I doubt whether this interpretation would have satisfied Paul either. I am convinced that the spiritual development he talks about in 2 Corinthians 4 comes through the very engagement with the rough and tumble of life rather than withdrawal from it. Growth surely comes from our discovery that God does sustain, whatever the physical or material circumstance. The glory of old age is in the ability it gives to reflect on our current experiences in the light of a lifetime of experience. It is surely not in a total withdrawal from everyday human experience.

(c) Old age as a period of personal witness to God's goodness
Ambrose writes:

'Old age is truly venerable when it grows hoary not with grey hairs, but with good deeds. The hoariness is revered, gleaming with shining thoughts and deeds.'

Again, the precise interpretation of how old people should express 'good deeds' or give witness to God's dealing with them varies from theologian to theologian. Richard Baxter, the seventeenth century English Puritan lists 15 'duties' of old age in his Christian Directory!

The basic argument is that older people are better able to understand God in that they have lived longer and have more experience of life. They are. therefore the most qualified to teach others about God and to pass on the inheritance of faith. This does not come automatically however, it needs discipline and guidance if the correct connections between life's experience and current circumstances are to be made. But old age certainly provides the potential for an active witness to the word and works of God, and older people have the wisdom to teach and encourage at both the personal, and also the community and political level. Those in later life have an important contribution to make to our development as a Christian community.

To consider these historic interpretations of ageing from the Christian tradition is important, even though in the context of the twentieth century these interpretations may not 'feel right' and may not form a coherent picture. Our task is to think through the meaning of old age for our generation. This is an exceedingly, complex exercise as I have indicated but a better theological understanding of what God intends by old age and what his will is for older people is essential if we are to understand how we might minister to, and work with those in later life. We have been given some excellent clues by our forefathers and it is important for us to continue the theological explorations.

4. WHO CARES FOR DEPENDENT OLDER PEOPLE?

Older women pensioners outnumber men by 2 : 1 and the vast majority of people over 85 years of age are women. The scenario of care for frail or ill older people at home overwhelmingly concerns women in their 60's or 70's caring for women (often mothers or mothers-in-law) in their 80's or 90's. Caring has been 'taken over' by women in the twentieth century and this is important in our understanding and response to old age.

As I write there is much discussion about the Government's White Paper on Caring for People (based on the report of Sir Roy Griffiths published in 1988) which envisages increasing care in the community. There is little doubt that public authority services in the future will be shaped towards encouraging people to live as normal a life a possible in their own homes or in the homes of relatives. But, just as care in residential homes inevitably means care by women, so in the vast majority of cases does care at home: care in the community will be largely women caring for women.

There is an erroneous assumption that vast numbers of older people live in residential homes or hospitals, but this is not the case. Although there has been a massive increase in the number of registered residential homes in the last decade, this has still not kept pace with the increase in the pensioner population. Approximately 4% of people over pensionable age live in residential home; the vast majority live in their own homes or with relatives or friends.

The conflicts in care
Looking after a relative can be a rewarding experience. It is often an exchange of love. But it can also become a limiting and exhausting task. Sometimes a difficult choice has to be made, whether to battle on with little help at the expense of one's own health and happiness or to seek a place in a residential home or hospital for one's relative or friend. On some occasions residential care is best but not inevitably so—most older people want to remain in their own homes, whatever the risks. Removal against their wish can have a devastating effect emotionally and sometimes irreparable damage is done to family relationships and there is an awful sense of guilt and shame amongst all involved.

Julia Johnson in her book *Day after Day: a guide to caring for an elderly relative*[1] lists a number of issues which need to be considered by anyone caring for an elderly relative.

The Christian minister may be called in to help people facing the conflict of caring and he or she might find it helpful to work through Johnson's check list with the carer.

[1] J. Johnson, *Day After Day: A guide to Caring for an Elderly Relative* (The Beth Johnson Foundation, Stoke-on-Trent, 1984).

Johnson's check list for carers:

Employment: Is looking after your relative depriving you of the social contact and creativity you find in your job? Is the work you do important to you financially and socially—is it important to your sense of well-being or independence—can you afford to give it up?

Finance: Are there extra financial demands being made on you as you meet your relative's needs and would these be adequately solved by admission to a residential home?

Social life: Are you unable to go out with relatives or friends or, if your relative lives with you, do you find it difficult to invite people to visit you at home?

Family life: Is there a lack of privacy both for yourself and for your relative? Do you find your care for your elderly relative affecting your marriage or your children's education or social lives too much?

Your health: Are you unable to attend to your own health needs because your relative's needs seem more pressing than your own? Are you anxious for much of the time and not sleeping well? Are you constantly tired? These are signs that you are feeling the strain of looking after your relative.

Stress: If you feel irritable with your relative and sometimes feel like hitting him or her ('granny battering' is far more common than we imagine and usually comes after many months of continuous caring by a loving daughter who is not coping with the stress); if you are tearful all the time and feel desperate; then you are under severe stress and need help quickly. It is not surprising if you are having to manage your relative day after day and perhaps without much sleep—but you must see a doctor and arrange for help. Don't be afraid to admit that you are not coping and need extra support. Don't be afraid to admit that care in a residential home may be the only realistic alternative, in spite of the complications.

Three other things need to be borne in mind:

i A transfer of power and authority will be taking place between the carer and the relative being cared for. Very often the carer is a daughter used to respecting the decisions of her parents.She will find it extremely difficult to go against their wishes and to make decisions about their lives for them. Some will not be able to do it at all, especially if their attitudes have been shaped by the command to honour their parents and not to usurp their authority. (I once counselled one man who could not discuss the removal of his mother to a residential home with her, because of her dominant attitude towards him, and eventually he had to write and tell her that he too agreed with those who recommended institutional care—it was a very painful time for mother and son and assistance with reconciliation and resolving of guilt were required for a number of months afterwards).

ii Older people have the right to make decisions about their lives. Sometimes the Christian minister will get torn between the expectations of the caring relative, desperately needing a break, and the expectations of the older person who will expect the minister to uphold his or her right to remain in control of their own lives. The negative attitudes which prevail in our society will urge us to side with the carer. However, we must not forget that we are also called to respect the wishes and decisions of the older person and to seek their growth and development as individuals. Both carer and cared for may be vulnerable and taking sides will not help.

iii Older people can only be removed from their homes against their will (by the public authorities) if they are a danger to themselves or others. If a people decide to remain at home they will need support in all aspects of their lives. Consideration needs to be given to the development of their spiritual lives, through house communion and prayer.

The encouragement of open conversations about how the carer and the older relative feel about each other and their respective situations always helps, but the readiness required to be honest with each other could take weeks of counselling at an individual level. The Christian minister is not there to take sides but to facilitate an interaction between the people involved which will enable decisions about the future to be taken, as far as possible with mutual agreement and without important relationships being broken. The minister should avoid being used as the spokesperson for the carer who is afraid to tackle the issue with her/his relative. The minister should be aware that the carer may want to offload the guilt felt at making a decision. It is far better, although more time-consuming, to facilitate a mutual sharing of issues and feelings and to seek a mutually agreed decision.

Institutional Care
Residential Homes and Nursing Homes for older people often provide a variety of services in addition to permanent care. Short stay care for a few weeks to give caring relatives a break can be provided, day care is sometimes available, and in some homes there is care just at night. These services will need to be explored and considered before any decision is made to transfer from home.

There are ways in which a move to an old people's home can be made less stressful for both the carer and the relative themselves.

Firstly, as already stated, the decision to move must have been made frankly and openly discussed and where possible a mutual agreement arrived at. Do not be afraid to allow the feelings the person being cared for has about residential homes to come out into the open and treat them with respect—older people's fears are often based on perceptions of residential care in the workhouse' as they knew it when they were young, and these fears need to be worked through. Loss of independence may be something else which will need to be tackled. Very few of us will find it easy to hand over decision-making about our lives.

During a visit to a residential home the carer and relative should look for:

   i The sort of bedroom provision made. Can a single room be provided? What personal furniture and belongings can be taken in? What rules are there about staying up late at night, or 'lying in' in the morning.

   ii The daily routine in the home. What freedoms and choices can be made by the residents? Is the home run on hierarchical lines or to a 'family group' model (where residents are encouraged to take on responsibilities for others in their group)? Are there regular visitors to the home and can residents go out, to the pub or to church?

   iii The staff; not just their qualifications, but their ability to relate to residents in a dignified way. Notice how the staff talk to and address the residents.

   iv Opportunities for visiting. Is the home on a suitable bus route to enable friends to visit?

   v If it is important for the older person—what provision is made at the home for spiritual development? Is there a place for quiet and prayer? Is there a regular celebration of the eucharist? Is there an opportunity for spiritual counselling?

It may be possible for a local church or housegroup to 'adopt' a group of residents in a local home. They could visit but could also arrange outings, visits or special events. Building relationships is vital for evangelism amongst older people and for encouraging openess amongst people to God and his word.

When a decision has been made about a particular home it may be possible for a short trial stay to be arranged. The more familiar a person is with the home, the less upsetting it will be when the permanent move is made. Remember that moving into a residential home means losing your own home, it may be a traumatic bereavement. Again, the Christian minister can assist here by helping all concerned recognize and come to terms with what is happening. This is especially important when the new resident complains about the home to a close relative and increases guilt. This is natural when people have experienced severe losses and can be coped with better when understood as such.

It is far better for possible problems or drawbacks in any home visited to be talked through, rather than that we should jolly the older person along by pretending that everything is fine.

5. INNOVATIVE MINISTRIES WITH OLDER PEOPLE

1. Celebrating Age: A programme to challenge myths and raise awareness

From my earliest days of ministry as Assistant Curate at St.Peter's, Rickerscote, Stafford, I have explored ways of improving, supporting and encouraging outreach to older people. I was encouraged by my Parish Priest to experiment with a series of educational activities designed to expose some of the myths about ageing and to change attitudes to old age. But first I needed to find out where the older people were and to gain their confidence.

I started with older church members. I visited a good number in their homes and joined in the regular activities of the older people's groups linked with the church. I spoke with other groups within the church about the needs of older people and about the opportunities of old age and challenged some to consider their attitudes towards ageing. For this I used the following group exercises:

. . . (A) Introducing reflection on attitudes:

(a) The 'adjectives' exercise:

   i List down the adjectives that readily come to mind when describing old age.

   ii Consider whether the list reflects a positive or negative view of old age.

   iii Ask whether the view reflects just the attitudes of the group of people present or society's view as a whole.

   iv Explore where the attitudes come from and how they are perpetuated.

   v Ask people to consider whether the list is an adequate description of the older people they know. Encourage people to think aloud about particular older people they know well to the rest of the group and to point up the differences from the initial list.

   vi Encourage the group to think why the list differs from so many individuals we know and to draw out and highlight the dangers of so easily assimilating generalizations about people.

This very simple exercise requires little preparation by the leader of the group but has proved to be an extremely stimulating method of promoting discussion about attitude formation and change—particularly amongst younger people).

(b) The 'photographs' exercise:

   i Ask the group to imagine they are going to produce a play for local festival.

ii Hand out a sheet of photographs (head shots) of people of different ages. (About 10 are needed). Explain that these people have submitted their photographs for the different characters of the play.

iii Ask the group to decide which one person they would choose for the following character list:
a company director
someone learning about computers
a person in love
a sailor (or rambler)
a deaf person
a lonely person
a politician
someone who is mentally ill
a poor person
someone who likes dancing

iv Explore with the group what caused them to choose particular people for particular parts. Consider the assumptions underlying their choices.

v Encourage the group to think about how our assumptions about people limit the opportunities and services we provide for them.

vi What we believe people to be will influence how we value them, how we value them will effect our attitude towards them, our attitude will determine what resources we make available for them and will dictate how we manage those resources.

vii Conclude with a discussion about the value of people in God's eyes.

This exercise is useful with older people's groups. The idea comes from the pack *Help Yourself to Health,* published by Pensioners Link and obtainable from Age Concern England.

I was eventually able to visit numerous older people who do not attend church and to obtain invitations to the nine 'Old People's Clubs' in the Parish and to the Sheltered Schemes to introduce discussions about attitudes (the church had already established good relationships with most of them in any case).

... (B) Preaching
At the same time I was seeking to explore attitudes and approaches to older people in my sermons Sunday by Sunday—on a number occasions I deliberately focussed on biblical characters who were older and used them to exemplify growth, determination, witness, prayer, strength and risk-taking. (e.g. Caleb, Hanna, Simeon, Anna, Paul) and on a couple of occasions I spoke deliberately about old age and our approaches to it.

... (C) A 'Celebrating Age' Weekend

All of this led up to a weekend of celebration sponsored by the church and called simply 'Celebrating Age'. A range of activities were planned with older people to give thanks for all that is good about growing older.

The Saturday events included:

— an art and craft display by older people

— a performance by an older people's choir from outside the parish

— presentations on diet and health

— two sessions on physical exercises suitable for older people

— an Health Education Unit presentation and display of videos

— a visible display of photographs and books on 'Stafford as we knew it'.

In the evening a special session was arranged under the title of 'Friendship with God in Later Life' when the Rev. Alan Eccleston (our special guest for the weekend) spoke of how he came to terms with and found great fulfilment in the experiences of later life lived in relationship with God.

The worship on Sunday was geared to the same theme and Alan Eccleston spoke on 'Prayer in Later Life'. The weekend was advertised widely and so many came on the Saturday afternoon that for some of the sessions there was standing room only (about 100 people). A number of enquiries were made after Alan's evening session and some people now join us for worship on a regular basis.

The Celebrating Age weekend resulted in a number of new initiatives being launched (in addition to providing lots of individual contacts). Hopefully it was a watershed in the thinking of the congregation about what old age is and how older people feel about life. It emphasized the positive aspects of a longer life without minimizing the difficulties.

2. Group Work with Older People: A programme for groups of older people in residential or day-care settings—based on reminiscence

As late as 1959 psychologists were advising their patients to avoid reminiscence, (Havinghurst 1959); however, since then, there has been a remarkable about-turn and the importance of memories as stimulants to creative thinking about the present and the future is now acknowledged:

'Memory is much more than the recall of past stimuli. It involves emotion, will and creativity in the reconstruction of the past to serve a person's present needs'.

(Coleman, 1986)

The recall of past experiences and the exercise of skills used long ago is now considered by many to be an important means of helping people retain their sense of identity. It helps people gain a sense of perspective on their life's history, it enables them to reflect on how their experiences have led them to be the sort of people they are now and with patient counselling can help them understand their behaviour in the context of their present conditions.

'A life lived reflectively by daily examination of experience will lead to a better life'.   (Laing)

Carl Jung, the psychoanalyst, argued that in later life people pursue 'religious questions' i.e. they search for meaning and purpose in life. We need to make sense of life's experiences; we search for a suitable framework in which the things that have happened to us can be set so we can see how they are linked and what they mean to the overall development of our lives. The recall of memories can trigger reflection and help people to gain this perspective on their lives.

I have devised a number of reminiscence programmes, some for use with relatively able people and some for use with quite physically or mentally frail people, I detail three of these programmes below:

(a) *A programme of guided reminiscence based on local history*
I have obtained books, photographs or items of memorabilia from the local library or individuals and encouraged conversation and discussion around these things. After the first session the group has been encouraged to bring their own items—they have always responded and sometimes overwhelmingly. On some occasions I have encouraged people to write about an experience and their feelings about it; on one occasion we even had poetry written. One woman of 94 years insisted on giving me a copy of her reflective poetry and prose, which I now treasure and am able to use with other groups. It is really not very difficult to encourage open discussion about people's histories, the skill is in making sure that everyone who wants to speak is given space to do so and in guiding the story-telling to some positive reflection. I have been involved in many exciting discussions with people written off as 'gaga' on subjects like the importance of loving relationships and the value of a relationship with God. We have discussed what people learnt in Sunday School and discovered seeds of faith which have begun to grow again.

(b) *The Help the Aged Recall material*
This is a professionally produced slide/tape presentation which records scenes, sounds and personal experiences from the 1920's onwards.

I have found the tapes to be particularly useful (in my opinion the slides are a distraction and inhibit discussion). There is a considerable amount of material which can lead to reflection of spiritual values (the tape opens with the hymn 'Jesus wants me for a Sunbeam!'). There is a section on the Second World War and recordings of important national events (like Edwards VIII's abdication speech). I have rarely

19

used more than a few minutes of a tape in each session and they have never failed to produce a stimulating sharing of personal stories with much meaningful reflection and analysis, even amongst people who are mentally frail.

(c) *The Quaker Questions*

i The group are invited to share their memories of what kept them warm during the winters when they were about 7 years old.

ii They are then asked to recall who they felt warm towards in their early life and why.

iii They are gently encouraged to share any experiences of God's warmth in their lives either as children or adults.

iv Friendly discussion is then encouraged about who or what makes them feel warm, now, where God's warmth is experienced in the present situation, especially in the Residential Home, Day Centre, Sheltered Housing Scheme.

The Quaker Questions are very much more directly geared towards evangelism and participants must be made aware from the start that there will be discussion about faith. The opportunities for sharing the gospel and helping people build their lives on their own declared experiences of God's love in their lives has been enormous. The Quaker Questions will need to be developed over a number of sessions of course—perhaps as many as six or even eight.

The reminiscence programmes, whilst being valuable in themselves, have sometimes led to more pastoral work at an individual level, sometimes at the request of a group member or because I have felt that things being shared by someone indicated a need for personal support or prayer. On one or two occasions I have found it necessary to provide longer term counselling, and here I have made use of the insights and practices of those involved in the ministry of 'healing of memories' and found that God has brought peace to minds where previously there was confusion or anger because of a particularly painful experience in earlier life. The reminiscence programmes have been a valuable means of extending the church's ministry amongst those who are frail and those who care for them.

3. Help Yourself to Health: A course designed to encourage self-help care amongst older people

The most important person in the maintenance of or the improving of an individual's health is themselves. He or she will decide when to attend the doctor's surgery or how rigorously they will implement a treatment regime prescribed by a doctor. They themselves will decide what sort of lifestyle they will lead, what food they will eat, what exercise they will take. Yet people are rarely taught how they might best approach these decisions or how they might cope with the stress which comes from making them.

Older people are constantly making critical decisions about their healthcare, although they may not see it in these terms. They rarely appreciate that the amount of mental stimulation they receive, the diet they maintain and the contact they have (or don't have) with others will influence their health either positively or negatively.

As a result of the interest in these things at the Celebrating Age weekend a course was held at St. Peter's which was designed to enable people explore how they could maintain or improve their health in the later years of their lives. The course was entitled *Help Yourself to Health* after the title of the course pack produced by Pensioners Link.

The outline for the course, which consisted of 12 sessions, was prepared after consultation with a number of local people although much of the material was adapted from the Pensioners Link pack.

The course was another means of the church offering something positive to the lives of older people, in addition to providing an opportunity for conversation and contact with people in an age group we were trying to serve. Sixteen people turned up at the first meeting but numbers soon settled to around 24-26 people per session. I would think the maximum number for this type of course would be 40. Titles for each course session included:

Why bother to keep fit

Increasing suppleness and strength

Listening to your body—how to relax and keep your blood pressure down

Tapping spiritual resources

Nothing beats meat and two veg—or does it?

Using your head—improving your memory

Handling the Doctor

What's involved in being a grandparent these days?

Pills, potions, and pains

The style was participatory, with much open discussion. Lots of use was made of quizzes, role play (without using the term), simple games and physical exercises. We shared a lot together and I felt it was important for the group not to be exposed to too many experts. We did invite a local community nurse to come and measure height, weight and blood pressure, and we did call on an expert on arthritis, and a leader for the exercise sessions, but I retained the leadership and provided the links from one week's session to the next.

The common theme from beginning to end was the importance of health and healing for the whole person, body, mind and spirit. There was therefore a natural opportunity to talk about the importance of a relationship with God to our own sense of of wellbeing. The session on Tapping Spiritual Resources attracted fewer people than had been attending for the few weeks previously but enabled the Parish Priest to speak about emotional healing through forgiveness, the value of prayer, the importance of symbols in helping us to come to terms with loss, the value of votive candles as a means of physically expressing deep feelings about life, love, hopes and fears. The session ended with people praying silently for each other's healing and wholeness through Christ. One person requested personal ministry afterwards, and others were obviously moved to think more deeply.

Whether the course was a success depends on where you stand to view it. A number of people joined a regular keep-fit class after the course and some joined our regular worshipping congregation and show a real commitment to Christ. Some we have not seen since.

4. Ministry and evangelism amongst individual older people
Ann Webber, in the booklet she prepared for a workshop at the National Evangelical Anglican Celebration in 1988 lists a number of important things to remember when ministering at a personal level to older people.

i Remember—older people have a diffferent perspective on time; they have no need to compete in the commercial world and so there is no need for them to rush. It is because we are out of touch with the natural rhythm of their life that we become frustrated. We need to be flexible and generous in the time we give to older people.

ii Remember—older people grew up with different social norms. Words that we take for granted now would have been taboo when the present generation of older people were young, and so we need to be careful in our use of language. Similarly, money and marital problems were discussed and managed in different ways by previous generations and many older people will feel confused by current thinking on these issues, e.g. hire purchase and divorce are still difficult for many older people to come to terms with.

iii Avoid being patronizing. Search for the creativity in the person and keep asking yourself 'where is God's image in this person or where are signs of his warmth?'

iv If a person has hearing difficulties make sure you speak with the light shining on your face; but don't assume that all older people have a hearing loss and need to be shouted at.

v Be prepared to help out with practical tasks like changing light bulbs.

vi Be prepared to listen to their life's experience and be open enough to be taught through listening and sharing.

vii If they have been active as Christians in the past, explore how contact with a church fellowship can be re-established. Transport may need to be provided or perhaps regular House Communion.

viii If you are visiting an older person living with relatives don't be diverted into talking to that person through the caring relatives. Persevere with direct communication, however frail or demented the person may appear to be.

ix If you are a clergyman, remember that for older people you will be a figure of power and authority. Maybe an informed member of your congregation could give better counsel on certain issues.

x If the person is mentally frail, remember they were still created in the image of God; give yourself the time to appreciate God's character within them, pay special attention to the consistencies in their conversation and build on these—certainly don't dismiss them as 'past it' when it comes to encouraging them to reach out to Jesus. Remember that the Holy Spirit ministers to the spirit of a person and can do so irrespective of the mind.

The gospel is best presented to frail older people at a personal level and within the security of a trusting relationship and a good relationship is often established through the provision of practical support and by listening. Again, with frail older people time is what is required.

In conversation watch particularly for feelings of regret, remorse or guilt about the past and give assurances of forgiveness in and through Jesus. Do not avoid discussion of death but be sensitive (in some parts of the country the parish priest is still known as the 'death man' amongst older people and a visit may be interpreted as a sign that life is soon to end). Do not misuse people's isolation and vulnerability, but respect their privacy and their decisions about their lives and their own eternal destiny—after all they are adults!

If our pastoral and evangelistic ministry to older people is to have integrity two things are essential in my view (and I've tried to reflect both of them in all that has been written in this booklet).

i We need to appreciate the prevalence and the effect of the negative attitude towards older people within our society—and that means within ourselves.

Prejudice is like the plague; just when you think you've got it under control it breaks out unexpectedly. We need constantly to be vigilant in our attack on ageism and to recognize its effects on older people.

It really cannot be satisfactory for us to present a gospel which encourages older people to withdraw from life and to prepare for death (although this may be wholly appropriate for a person suffering from a terminal illness). Neither is it satisfactory to reduce our ministry to the patronizing provision of free handouts or cheap trips to the pantomime at Christmas. If the gospel has to do with New Life we should be encouraging older people to explore their potential for creative activity, for maintaining and improving their health, and for establishing or re-establishing loving relationships with other people and with God. We should be providing opportunities for the development of understanding, growth and experimentation. A positive approach to the potentialities of old age will motivate us as ministers and will ensure that the necessary resources are made available for the provision of creative opportunities.

ii We need to think in holisitic terms. Later life, perhaps more than any other period of our lives, provides the opportunity for reflection and the integration of our self-understanding. Helping older people to see the interactions between physical, social, economic, mental and spiritual aspects of their lives is vitally important if we are to expect them to respect our message or appreciate our concern. It really cannot be satisfactory to minister to older people as though their former life is of no consequence to their present circumstances. An appreciation of an an individual's life span is an essential prerequisite to an effective ministry with older people, it is far better to encourage people to see where God has been working in their lives over the years through love, through their creativity and through hope and to encourage them to see how these were epitomized in Jesus than to dismiss their life experience as unimportant or even inconsequential in the sight of God as I have heard some do.

The practical activities described in this booklet are based on these two fundamental attitudes, they provide scope for reflection on life's experiences and emphasize the positive aspects of growing older which a relationship with God in Christ can enhance. They appear to me to be effective structures through which personal ministry and evangelism can take place, they provide frameworks through which people can share their hopes and fears and in which a witness can be given to a personal experience of God through knowing Jesus.